junk style

junk style

Melanie Molesworth

photography by **Tom Leighton**

Stewart, Tabori & Chang

New York

First published in 1998 by
Ryland Peters & Small
Cavendish House
51–55 Mortimer Street
London W1N 7TD

Published in 1998 and distributed in the U.S. by Stewart, Tabori & Chang,
a division of U.S. Media Holdings, Inc.
115 West 18th Street, New York, NY 10011

Distributed in Canada by
General Publishing Company Ltd.
30 Lesmills Road
Don Mills, Ontario, Canada M3B 2T6

Library of Congress Cataloging-in-Publication Data
Molesworth, Melanie
    Junk Style/Melanie Molesworth;
photography by Tom Leighton
        p.   cm.
    Includes bibliographical reference and index.
    ISBN 1-55670-653-7
    1. House furnishings. 2. Interior decoration. 3. Secondhand trade. 4. Junk trade. I Title
TX311.M65 1998
645-dc21   97-31725
                                   CIP

Printed in China

10 9 8 7 6 5 4 3 2 1

4

Contents

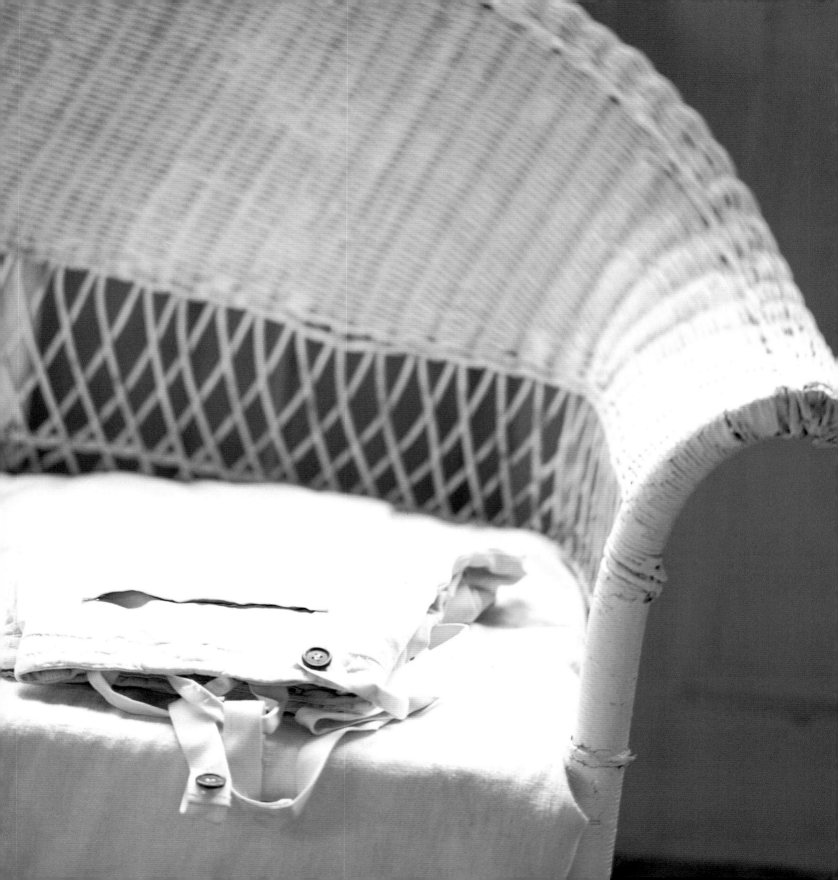

introduction

This book is proof that one person's junk is another's treasure. It's all about doing new, unexpected, and stylish things with objects that would otherwise be thrown away or forgotten. It means choosing possessions that have already had a life and have already been loved instead of ones that are new, pristine, and soulless. It involves accepting cracks, chips, and blemishes as part of an item's attraction and as evidence that it is unique. It requires you to forget how much or how little something costs.

Though the term "junk" describes anything that has been discarded, some so-called trash is too good to be consigned to dumpsters. Many pieces cry out to be recycled and reintegrated into our homes. Discerning devotees of junk style pick these pieces from among the clutter, upgrade them, and incorporate their timeless qualities into their lives.

hunting out treasures above

Be warned. There's a fine line between being the first to pick a bargain and being the idiot who goes home to live with a dud.

recognizing potential opposite

Imagine a place for each piece before you buy, and think beyond traditional uses—a metal bucket could hold firewood, for example.

The photographs in this book show real homes filled with all manner of recycled pieces that are unfailingly chic and elegant. The owners have embraced the idea of junk collecting so wholeheartedly they spend weekends searching for more examples of faded beauty. For them, using junk is a way of life. Indeed, much of this look's appeal is that you can't just go and buy it off the shelf. The hunt itself is half the fun. Flea markets, antiques fairs, tailgate sales, salvage yards, estate sales, office clearance sales, auctions, thrift shops, and secondhand stores all reveal finds from the exceptional to the ordinary. Each source is unpredictable and offers its own secrets: What you end up with depends on where you look, when you get there, and what your tastes are. You don't need the skills of a knowledgeable antiques dealer to pick up bargains. The secret is simply to look for something that particularly appeals to you—a texture, a subtly aged color, skillful craftsmanship, a decorative flourish, or an object's practicality—and to make a purchase based on esthetic considerations, not price or provenance. Salvaged items sourced with care, restored with love, and introduced to your home with flair will always be its most interesting and expressive pieces. Don't be afraid to put a contemporary spin on whatever you find, mixing old with new in ways that reflect your own personal style. Happy hunting!

inspirational finds

color

The best foil for junk style is almost always white: Its sheer simplicity and clean, timeless look provide the perfect contemporary background for any type of junk furniture, from polished dark wood tables to classic 1950s sofas in jazzily colored slipcovers. Often a judicious injection of strong color used as an accent on paintwork can add vibrancy to an otherwise cool scheme.

bright colors left

Yellow paint and cream walls set off the strong shapes of carefully chosen furniture.

highlights right

One stong color on the ceiling gives this bathroom an edge.

But choosing the right shade is vital. Harsh tones can overpower the subtlety of natural materials and dominate organic pigments that have been gradually dulled by the bleaching effect of the sun and a lifetime of cleaning and wear and tear. Muted shades that mimic the natural effect of aging, such as pale pastels or earthy tonés of terra-cotta, can offer the best complement.

muted shades **right**

The mood of a room can be dictated by the color scheme. The calm, restful atmosphere of this old Long Island barn is enhanced by the subtle shades chosen for the paint on the walls and the furniture.

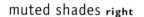

metallics **left**

This Paris apartment has been brought up to date with white paint and an eclectic mix of metal furniture. The pickled finish on the old wooden beams and the floor-boards echoes the chalky patina of weathered metal.

hot colors **far right**

*The 1950s epitomized bright
jazzy colors. Here classic
Robin Day—designed chairs in
burnt orange sit alongside
other 1950s furniture.*

cupboards **right/below**

*Bold use of strong color can
make a feature of individual
items of furniture.*

Surfaces touched by the gentle aging process are some-thing special that you inherit rather than buy, and that's why the imperfections characteristic of junk furniture and other salvaged possessions are so precious. Peeling wallpaper, rough plaster walls, exposed bricks, flaking paint on a door, a rusty headboard, some worn-out rugs, a bare wood tabletop, and flagstones pol-ished by decades of footsteps should all be cherished because many years of use have made them that way. In deference to this, crumbling walls can be left undecorated, the cracked or dusty bare brick setting the tone for the surroundings in which you keep your junk-shop finds. For flooring, simplicity is the best approach. Bare boards, sanded down and then either polished with beeswax or pickled for a paler, more contemporary look, are an economical and practical option for virtually every room.

surfaces

peeling paper right

A hallway with remnants of 1950s wallpaper frames a casual still life of garden paraphernalia.

the rough with the smooth left

Cracked tiles make a practical floor; a rough wall with a road sign brings the outside in; old floor-boards are brought up to date; years of peeled paint create an inimitable effect.

original walls **right**

In this guest bedroom the owners have left the walls unrenovated, so that the overall look is a collage of different textures.

20

Look out also for reclaimed flagstones and tiles at architectural salvage yards. Ceramic tiles bought in small batches might not be enough to cover a whole floor, but they can be incorporated into larger-scale designs or used to create a fire-place or a border around a sink. Cracked or incomplete tiles are useful, too—they can be broken up and laid down to tessellate an area of floor for the ultimate in waste not, want not.

On walls, old layers of wallpaper and paint can be partially scraped back to reveal the decors chosen by generations of previous occupants. Alternatively, you might chance upon some unopened rolls of old wallpaper in an estate sale and decide to use them to conjure up the style of another era.

pattern on pattern left

*Sections of flaking 19th-century
wallpaper still cling to the walls
alongside layers of paint and
plaster, revealing the choices of
colors and designs of all the
previous owners of the house.
The painted fireplace is
similarly unrenovated.*

furniture
and furnishings

Whether you are looking for something handsome or quirky, decorative or functional, industrial or domestic, ornate or unadorned, antique or contemporary—or a mix of all of them— the joy of junk furniture is that there's something for everyone. A house filled with junk furniture will have a wonderfully timeless feel, so scour sales and markets for pieces that fit in with your home's unique style. As you become accustomed to shopping in this sort of environment, where a beautiful cabinet might be nestling underneath a pile of old wooden boxes, you'll become adept at selecting interesting items from among the mundane.

geometric lines above

The angular lines of a classic Robin Day armchair create a sharp, boxy shape.

James Bond style right

This white metal swivel chair was bought inexpensively from an office-furniture warehouse.

outside in

An old weathered garden bench was chosen for its simple curved lines and crusted paint surface.

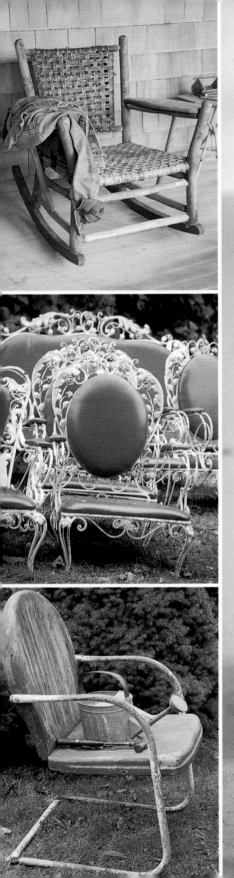

chairs

all shapes and sizes

left to right

Junk chairs come in every imaginable style: A slatted old French folding chair makes a great spare seat for impromptu guests; an old rocker sits on a beachhouse deck; fancy metal seats wait to be sold at Ruby Beet's junk lovers' paradise on Long Island; a worn chair awaits a home outside Potted Gardens store in New York; raffia chairs face the sea; a folding chair makes a useful garden table; unusual shapes form a splintery chair; a sandblasted metal chair has urban style.

Junk shops and flea markets are filled with a wealth of chairs that have all stood the test of time. You are almost certain to strike it lucky, whether you are searching for an assortment of seating for the dining room, a dressing-table stool, some metal garden furniture, or a cozy armchair. Try each piece for size before you buy, and look for indications that the chair has been comfortable enough to have been well used in the past—the sagging seat of an armchair or a wooden armrest that shines from years of use are both good signs, so don't be deterred by them. And anyway, quick and easy alterations such as a new cover, some plump pillows, or a simple fabric throw will easily hide any major imperfections if the basic character of the piece is right.

slatted style left/right

*A casual arrangement of
furniture gleaned from the
garden looks surprisingly
elegant in an Amsterdam loft.*

If you are on the lookout for dining-room or kitchen chairs, it is unlikely that you will come across a complete matching set in a junk store. Instead, consider buying an assortment of single chairs as and when you see them, and gradually build up an idiosyncratic selection of your own. Look for examples that have arms and gently sloping high backs for ultimate comfort as you dine, and make tie-on seat cushions from scraps of fabric from the flea market to soften their look as well as their feel. You'll find that your guests are so comfortable they will want to linger around the table long after the meal is over.

Wicker tub chairs and metal garden chairs—especially folding slatted ones that can be stored flat and then pressed into service if you have unexpected guests—are all worth considering, along with more conventional ladderbacks. Old wooden chairs taken

park chairs left

*Metal-framed wooden chairs,
like these at an antiques fair,
can make a similarly stylish
set of dining chairs.*

28

elegance left

Beautiful enough to be used purely for decoration, this pale wooden chair is placed in the best light to show off its glowing color and attractive curves.

solidity right

Some chairs are so sturdily constructed you know they have years more of useful life in them, like this chunky box-seated chair.

versatility left

You don't have to use chairs only as seats—placed at convenient points, they can make useful extra surfaces.

character right

Some chairs you just fall in love with for a detail, such as a studded leather seat.

from old meeting halls and schoolrooms often crop up in junk stores alongside tall laboratory stools and rush-seated café chairs. All are perfect for kitchen seating as they are particularly sturdily made and are often stackable, a real asset if you are short of space.

Elegant one-of-a-kind items such as rockers and woven Lloyd Loom chairs will be at home in a bedroom or bathroom, creating a quiet corner in which to relax. For workrooms and studies, office-furniture clearance sales are good sources of seating—adjustable architects' chairs and leather swivel chairs are practical as well as better looking and more unusual than modern options. Make sure you buy one that is the correct height for use with your desk. You want to be able to work in comfort as well as style.

the main feature

A kitsch 1950s chair becomes
a focal point in the corner of
this otherwise minimally
decorated apartment.

benches
and sofas

Buying a new sofa is an expensive business, so a junk-store alternative, even if it needs a few repairs, is an exceptionally good buy. Metal-framed daybeds, benches, and chaise longues are also much sought because they are sociable pieces of furniture that give a room an air of casual relaxation, especially when piled high with an inviting assortment of pillows or strewn with an old rug or afghan.

A generous seating arrangement is a must in the living room, but is also wonderful in the sort of kitchen that is the hub of family life, a quiet bedroom where you might retreat with a book, a corner of a roomy bathroom, or as a much-needed place of rest in a study. Whichever part of the house the sofa is destined for, comfort should be your priority when you are on the lookout for the best buys. Sprawl out on sofas before you part with any money to make sure they are as comfortable as they are good looking. To make sure that wooden, wicker, and metal-framed benches meet the same criteria, buy and fit some feather-filled squab cushions. The bench can then be used as overflow seating in the living room or space-saving seating alongside a rectangular dining table—perfect for children to use at family meals.

sackcloth far left

The pillows and squab cushions for this bench have been designed to set off the stitched strip and logo on these old French flour sacks.

reinventing the wheel above/left

An old cart wheel rescued from a sale of farming implements becomes a work of art when it is placed in an interior setting.

cover story above

*Sturdy cream linen sheets
help protect a generous sofa
from the rigors of family life
in this Dutch living room.*

32

Leather-covered couches age beautifully and are lucky flea-market finds that may need only the odd patch here and there to make then serviceable. Along with classic Knoles and Chesterfields, they are the ultimate in shabby chic. To hide leaking stuffing or a cover that is too worn to leave on show, make some slipcovers from a fabric that will complement the couch's faded look or shroud the whole thing in a large swathe of cloth: Ignore folds and creases and simply tuck in the edges. Search out faded curtains, sacking cloth, and bedspreads with a lived-in look, and your "new" upholstery will not detract from the couch's dated charm.

creased up **right**

Any old couch can be given a

new lease on life with a sim-

ple cream cover, as long as

the framework is sound.

bright white

White unifies this eclectic mix of junk furniture for a '90s look. The decorative fluted legs of the table contrast with the plain circular top.

tables

Forget convention and use flea-market finds ranging from old cable reels to large trunks as tables. Add a scrubbed plank bench, a simple trestle, a delicate wire-work console, and you'll realize that junk stores can provide every surface you will ever need, from dining tables and bed-side cabinets to makeshift desks.

For kitchens it's hard to beat old pine refectory tables, which are easy to find in all shapes and sizes. They are extremely practical, and with a thick coat of tough varnish they can withstand the rigors of hot pans as well as the children's crayons. Go for the biggest size your kitchen can accommodate, as this surface is likely to be used for letter writing, hobbies, and reading the newspaper as well as at meal-times and for food preparation. If your space is too limited to hold this sort of expansive surface, drop-leaf tables are more versatile. They can accommodate larger gatherings when necessary, while those with drawers are useful for extra storage. Small steel-topped tables and butcher's blocks are also good for pro-viding an extra work surface when space is at a premium.

Even if your kitchen is on the small side, you can look for a pretty marble-topped café table with cast-iron legs or a small wicker table that will fit snugly into

sweet dreams

An old garden table with twisted metal legs works just as well beside a bed.

a corner and be big enough for two people to eat there comfortably. It's also useful to have a small table in the hallway on which to keep keys and mail, place a lamp, or display a generous vase of fresh flowers for an immediate welcome. Try to find an unusual piece of furniture that will make a striking first impression: a sewing-machine bench, an ornate metal-framed table with a glass top, or a decorative wooden console will establish the junk-style look as soon as you step inside the front door.

Occasional tables are indispensable in the living room for taking tea by the fire or keeping your book beside a favorite armchair, so search secondhand stores and garage sales for anything from small wooden stools and folding butler's tray tables to wooden tea trolleys and stacking coffee tables.

Many of these options are also good to use beside the bed in preference to conventional matching cabinets, or in the bathroom piled with fresh linens or baskets of soaps. And if you unearth something at a flea market that really has passed its best but still has some quality about it that appeals to you, there's a good chance that it will still come in handy in the yard or potting shed as a workbench or a plant stand.

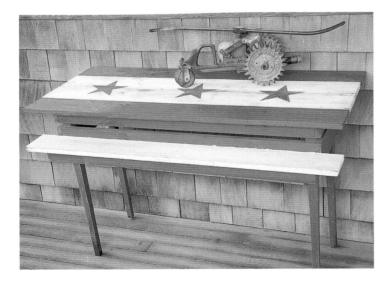

recycling left/right

A huge cable wheel becomes a fashion designer's worktable in a Paris apartment, while a sewing-machine stand complete with foot pedal makes an unusual side table.

stars and stripes far left

National pride obviously dictated the decoration for this brightly painted two-tier table.

lucky find left

A simple trestle is the most basic table you will find; it is a versatile shape that will work well in any situation.

piano cover **left**

*A pretty striped cotton in
French blue helps disguise a
piano, and contrasts with blue
checks on the chair.*

fabrics

Junk stores are filled with textiles such as curtains, blankets, mattress ticking,

quilts, bed linens, lace, and fabric remnants of all sizes in innumerable colors, weights,

textures, and patterns. The inimitable look and feel of faded chintz, old velvet, time-

softened linens, and kitsch prints will make your rooms feel snug and lived in, so blend

together a variety of these fabrics, mixing them with modern pieces if you like. Use more

precious pieces sparingly in a position where they can take pride of place and allow less

costly ones to hang in generous folds. Vintage fabrics can be left unironed, threadbare, or

patched to give your surroundings an air of relaxed living.

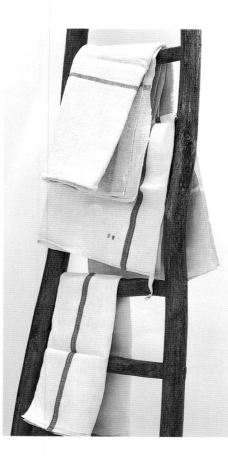

ticking over **left**

*Traditional mattress ticking comes in a
huge range of colors and looks great
mixed up on this wrought-iron bed.*

ladder of success **right**

*An old ladder propped up against a wall
makes an original towel rail in the
bathroom or the kitchen.*

Vintage fabrics have a charm that cannot be replicated by modern material, however faithful fabric companies may be in copying old designs. The fabrics that survive years of good service relatively intact tend to be the durable ones, and are usually made from natural fibers rather than synthetics, an appropriate complement to the other natural textures, such as wood, that recur in junk style. The authentic feel of antique linen or lace or soft wool blankets that have been washed so many times the nap has worn smooth, more than compensates for a frayed edge or occasional small hole. Paisley, florals,

40

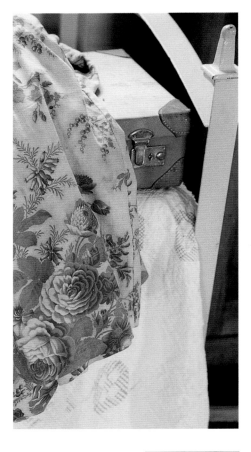

a touch of lace **above**

Recycled drapes also provide

a delicate lacy undersheet

beneath the top cover.

rambling roses **below**

Blowsy rose drapes spread

over a dormitory bed trans-

form the mood of the room.

stripes, and checks are a useful way to bring a splash of pattern to otherwise subtly decorated rooms, often inspiring their overall color schemes. Even the most overblown chintz will look charming rather than overpowering when surrounded by the casual restraint of junk style. So drape dining tables with layers of linen and lace for a touch of faded grandeur, dress beds with antique linens, soft quilts, and feather-filled pillows, cover sofas and chairs with fabrics such as sensual silk, knobbly chenille, starched cotton, and warm wool to enhance their comfortable appeal.

floral charm **below**

This pretty bed cover is a curtain found in a country junk store's rummage basket.

violets **above**

Subtle florals, like this 1950s design, can soften an otherwise coolly decorated room.

pure white **below/right**

All-white bed linen lends a monastic feel. If you need extra warmth, it's a simple matter to add layers of soft woolen blankets, as the owner of this 19th-century wrought-iron folding traveling bed has done.

picnic checks **opposite**

Old faded woolen blankets in contrasting pale pastels were used to reupholster this pair of classic armchairs with rounded arms. They are soft, comfortable oases in a minimally furnished London loft.

42

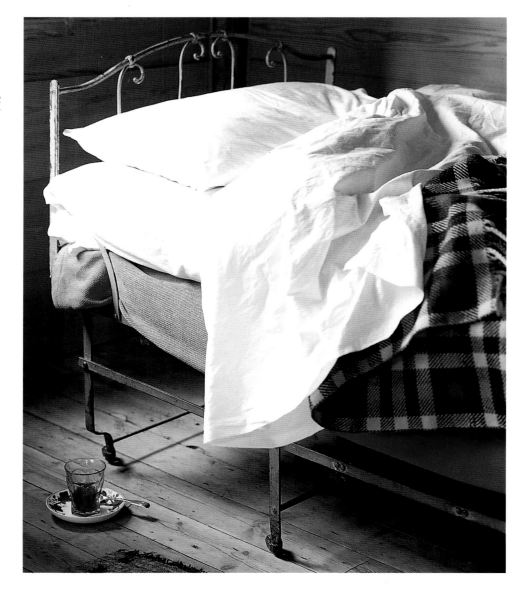

To complement rich vintage textiles, buy new lengths of utility fabrics such as cotton ticking, gingham, sheeting, muslin, and tough canvas. They are cheap enough to use in large quantities, made into slip-covers or sewn into a border to make a small, treasured piece of fabric a more workable size, and because they are timeless they blend well with older, more decorative fabrics. Try mixing new gingham with a faded floral, pristine ticking with some old checks, an elegant damask with some unbleached cotton, or a length of linen with a panel of antique embroidered lace. And when you have finished sewing, do what generations have done before you—collect any leftover scraps to make into a patchwork quilt.

pots of style opposite

*Kitchen scales and salt pots
sit among storage jars and
bottles in a monochrome
collection of kitchenware.*

boxed in left

*Plenty of dents and a rusty,
peeling-paint finish simply
add to the charm of these
old storage tins.*

containers

and storage

For innovative storage solutions, junk stores make wonderful hunting grounds. From boxes and baskets to cabinets and shelving, these pieces are essential additions to any well-organized home, whether you like to maintain a minimalist, clean, and contemporary look or to fill your home with a wonderful array of treasured clutter. Search for both conventional and unsual pieces to house your possessions. Useful finds include enameled tins and bread boxes, wooden crates, medicine chests, baker's racks, butcher's hooks, and an assortment of basketware.

great crates right

*Baskets and wine crates complete with
original lettering are an economical and smart
storage solution for a Paris apartment.*

small storage

Before the days of mass production and man-made materials, people took great care to market everything from vegetables to soap powder in tins, trays, bags, crates, racks, barrels, boxes, and baskets that were carefully packaged and often labeled with beautiful lettering to advertise their contents and the producer's identity. They were so durably made that many still survive today, frequently cropping up among the junk at stands and markets after years of being shut away in attics and cellars. All deserve to be given a new lease on life, so buy them to use for storage all around the home as well as outdoors. They are far more desirable than the crude replica tins and baskets that are now on the market in response to a revived interest in period pieces.

Wooden grocery trays and vegetable crates are useful for storing toys in a playroom, displaying plants in a sunroom, growing herbs on the kitchen windowsill, and holding supplies of dried goods in the kitchen. Brightly painted logos, especially ones that reveal an exotic past, are most sought after. Old shopping bags and baskets, bicycle bags, picnic hampers, and fisherman's baskets are coveted for their

46

enamelware right

Enameled kitchenware, very popular in the 1930s, is still going strong today.

egg box left

A metal box originally used to store eggs has found a new home as a place to keep paperwork and letters.

48

intricate workmanship as well as for their versatility. Fill them with shoes to store under the bed, with logs to sit beside the fireplace, or line them with fabric and use them for laundry. A fraying handle or a unraveled edge can be either carefully repaired or left as it is to add to the charm.

Enameled tins often appear among kitchenalia in junk stores—sometimes labeled "flour" or "sugar," sometimes striped or with colored lids. French versions of these canisters, in which to keep *farine* and *sucre*, are particularly sought after for recreating rural Provençal style or faded Parisian chic. A mismatched assortment of these tins looks wonderful on a kitchen shelf and are just as useful today as they were originally.

well dressed **above**

A utilitarian metal rod is a perfect makeshift wardrobe, allowing a wonderful array of secondhand clothes to be on permanent show.

birdhouses **right**

A row of narrow wooden bird-houses sits on top of a basic set of painted wooden drawers. If some drawers in a unit are missing, utilize the empty spaces for displaying favorite objects.

over a barrel **right**

Barrels at Fish's Eddy pottery store in New York wait to be recycled as anything from umbrella stands to laundry baskets.

baskets **far right**

Baskets are handy all around the house—store bulbs in the potting shed, vegetables in the kitchen, or even house sleeping kittens.

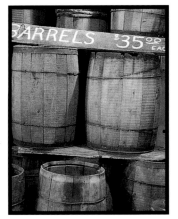

Metal trunks, old suitcases, and leather collar and hat boxes can be filled with clothes, books, and papers, then piled on top of a chest or under a dresser to create an attractive display as well as making the most of limited space and reviving an age-old household practice. For bathrooms, search for wooden drying racks, linen chests, and laundry baskets to store towels, and small shelving units, glass bottles, and small baskets for toiletries. Map chests, bookcases of all shapes and sizes, and wooden crates are ideal for books and magazines and also to hold the accumulations of modern life that add unnecessary clutter to the clean lines of the junk-style look, such as records and compact discs. A metal filing cabinet will swallow up all those household papers,

good read **below far left**

A collection of books and glassware is enticingly displayed on open shelves.

kept on file **below left**

Metal filing-card boxes are indispensable for the home office or workroom.

garden display **below**

A rickety wooden baker's stand is an attractive addition to a sheltered corner of the yard. It is a convenient place to keep tools and equipment and to display fruit and vegetables freshly picked from the kitchen garden.

50

herb garden **left**

For a handy kitchen garden, drill

holes in the base of a wooden

crate and plant it with a variety

of culinary herbs.

portable **below**

A shallow-sided crate can be

used as an impromptu tray.

bills, and documents. Glass-fronted cabinets and open shelves are indispensable all around the house, and recycled store display furniture, such as large wooden notions display counters with glass-fronted drawers, makes really original storage units. In the bedroom it's hard to beat freestanding metal clothes rods, blanket chests, old leather suitcases, and even dressmaker's dummies for original and truly stylish storage.

In awkward spaces such as halls, try pegs, hat stands, drawstring shoe bags, and metal shelving, or look for old paneled wooden doors at flea markets; they can be set over existing alcoves and recesses—for example, under the stairs—to make extra cupboards that look as if they have been there for years. Equip them with shelves or rows of hooks, and they are the ideal place to store linen, coats, and household equipment.

52

to the home, especially in the bedroom, where a large freestanding French-style armoire or a rough-and-ready pine one can be wonderfully stylish. Corner cabinets allow you to make the most of space that would otherwise be wasted. Details like ornate carving, decorative molding, colored-glass insets, a mirrored front panel, and attractive hardware all make a purchase worthwhile.

Easier to carry back from your foray are smaller cupboards, which are useful throughout the house for storing anything from clothes and stationery to food. Glass-fronted cabinets are ideal if

cupboards

cupboard love **above**

An ornate, painted wall cupboard is lined with illustrations taken from an old recipe book.

With a little imagination, the cupboards you can find in flea markets and at auctions are simply the starting point for ingenious, attractive large-scale storage. For example, a painted metal kitchen cabinet, would make a convenient place to store dishes, an armoire could become a pantry, and a small wooden kitchen hutch could find a new role in the bathroom stacked high with towels.

Generously proportioned cupboards can be practical and handsome additions

you are happy to put the contents of the cupboard on show. Arrange what's inside attractively—whether it is toiletries, cans of baked beans, or your best crockery—to make the most of the display.

Revamping your cupboards with new or reclaimed doorknobs, handles, and decorative and unusual brass or iron hinges, or even just polishing up the existing ones with steel wool, can work wonders. Equally effective for transforming the ordinary into something special is replacing cracked or warped door panels with etched or clear glass, chicken wire, or a length of fabric gathered on a wire.

53

very cool above

Stripped of its enameled surface, a classic refrigerator shows off its sleek lines in bright stainless steel.

classic left/far left

A simple cupboard furnishes a guest room with extra storage—if you are looking for something similar flea markets and yard sales provide plenty of choice.

picture of style above

Pale colors fill the home of French designer Roxanne Beis, and this subtly bleached, metal-trimmed cupboard fits in perfectly.

in the garden left

No junk item should be too precious for outdoor life—this handsome flower-topped armoire graces a patio.

lamps
and lighting

Lighting has a huge impact on the way we feel about a room and the way we see the possessions that fill it. Even the no-frills approach of a simply shaded bulb or a naked candle flame has a profound effect on its atmosphere. So when you are creating a specific look from your junk-store finds, it is important that you don't ignore details such as lighting. While there is no need to slavishly keep to one style or period, you should strive to be sympathetic to the overall look, and many modern light fixtures will jar horribly. Install decorative light fixtures that have been gleaned from your favorite shops and markets instead and they will add to the overall character of junk style.

rise and fall

This elegant, adjustable hanging light proves that you don't have to choose a modern fixture for versatility.

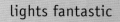

lights fantastic

Search flea markets for period light fixtures such as wirework candleholders, a French glass shade to hang over a dining table, or a clip-on metal spot lamp that is perfect for task lighting in the kitchen.

Salvage yards and secondhand stores are usually well stocked with a range of original light fixtures, many of which have been removed from old houses in the name of modernization. But some of these items are still fully functional and can last another lifetime if they are rescued and reused. The only thing to remember is that secondhand electric-light fixtures should always be checked and installed by a qualified electrician, so that any worn or damaged wiring or connections can be replaced. Once their safety has been certified, old fixtures will do their job far more stylishly than their modern equivalents, which are often too high-tech in style and form to sit easily beside the other more traditional elements in your home.

The warmth and romance of candlelight fit in perfectly with the relaxed nature of junk style, so use it wherever possible. Candle holders can come in many different forms, from containers designed specifically for the job to old pots and jars adapted for the purpose. For a decorative flourish, old pewter candlesticks, perhaps dented or worn smooth by years of polishing, can often be found relatively cheaply among more expensive antiques. Rustic-style options include storm lanterns and sturdy metal hurricane lamps, which look great on the mantelpiece or table, but which are also useful outside on summer evenings.

a good sign right

In addition to buying old lights, you can adapt other junk items to camouflage modern light fixtures. This highly original wall light fixture was made from an old rusted metal road sign. The bulb behind floods the wall with light.

56

candlelight **below**

A row of thick glass storm lanterns are suspended from a beam to provide a warm glow on a dark night.

on the road **bottom**

A metal roadworker's' lamp finds a new use lighting dining tables in Woolloomooloo restaurant in Avignon.

storm front **bottom**

Whether used purely for decoration or to light an alfresco meal, hurricane lamps are romantic and stylish.

display only **below**

A small round mirror reflects the rusted metal wick control of an old gas-light fixture with its original glass lantern..

Before you head off on your first foraging expedition, plan the lighting scheme for each room in the house, deciding what type and style of fixtures you need and where they will go. Each room should have something to provide general or ambient lighting —a central hanging light, for example. There should also be individual task lights over desks, beside armchairs, and in kitchens to make studying, reading, or cooking easier. Finally, you will need some sort of accent lighting to draw the eye toward particular areas that you wish

take the floor **below**

An ornate floor lamp beside an open fire is the ideal place to relax with a good book and a model of a dog to provide silent company.

to highlight, such as a work of art or an attractive collection of objects on display. Lighting to fulfill all these roles—plus any pieces you fall in love with on the spot for their purely decorative qualities and elect to find a place for as soon as you return home—can easily be found by sifting through junk stores.

Finding a colored or plain glass-drop chandelier might well be one of the highlights of your search—with a bit of cleaning and perhaps a replacement glass drop here and there, it will give off a delicate twinkling light that is grand but never gaudy. Hang it in conventional style over a dining table or somewhere more unusual, such as a bathroom, to give an air of opulence. You may even decide to use a chandelier purely as a beautifully decorative object and not have it wired to the electricity supply for use as a light. If this is the case, it should be hung near a source of natural light, such as a window, so the glass drops catch and reflect all available sunlight. Candelabras make a similarly grand statement, but remember that lighted candles should never be left unattended and that the smoke can stain painted walls and ceilings.

Look out, too, for glass or ceramic uplighters that will wash an entire wall with gentle light, and for elegant standard lamps, with or without their original shades. Pleated shades to fit—silk if you are lucky, paper if you are not—can often be found separately, along with an assortment of other shades in glass, metal, parchment, wicker, or fabric. These can either be paired with other lamp bases you might find or easily adapted to use with hanging fixtures. Wall sconces—some incorporating candleholders, others equipped with kitsch flame-shaped bulbs—are also much sought after, especially wrought-iron models in ornate floral or foliage designs. The best finds are always the classic designs, and in the case of lighting these are old adjustable gooseneck desk lamps, tall metal standing lamps with extending arms, and traditional brass picture lights.

59

clear your desk **top**

Yard sales are good sources for adjustable desk lamps. Check that the springs are sound—too tight and the lamp won't budge, too loose and the lamp will flop.

workstation **above**

Gooseneck lamps are essential desk accessories in traditional or contemporary offices—their flexible and stylish design has changed little over the years.

mix and match left

Look for assorted pieces of cheap glassware and flatware for everyday use.

glass, china,
and ceramics

decoration opposite

A selection of intricately patterned spoons, some tied in a bundle with blue wool, makes a pretty still life on an ornate glass dish. Though the flatware is mismatched, the styles are similar enough to make a harmonious whole.

something special right

Glass vases, dishes, and cake plates are useful one-of-a-kind purchases. They might seem kitsch in isolation, but together they make a charming group.

The delicate floral china plates and cut-glass vases that were last cherished by our grandmothers are now fashionable once again and are an integral part of junk style. Think of a cream pitcher filled with flowers, a china bowl planted with hyacinths, a shelf laden with dishes, a table piled high with earthenware, or a tea tray set with bone china and you'll capture the right look. Prices are very reasonable, so it is easy to build up an impressively diverse collection for everyday use or for decorative purposes. Rifling through piles of plates, searching for a saucer to match a cup, and imagining how a bottle would look after a cleaning, merely adds to the enjoyment.

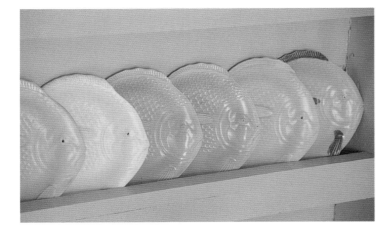

Gone are the days when we had to have a fully matching dinner set. Now, table settings with character can include mismatched plates, odd glasses, and an assortment of flatware, even for entertaining. Whether you are hosting a dinner party or just having friends for morning coffee, a casual assortment of glass and china will make it a welcoming and easygoing affair.

Tableware makes up only a fraction of the pieces you are likely to come across. If you spot a bowl and pitcher set, a dish, or some dresser china, your junk-store finds could also adorn

all set right

Among more ordinary china you may be lucky enough to find a complete dinner set.

shelf life left

Simple wooden shelving is the perfect place to display china plates amassed over many years.

fishy top far left

This collection of china has a seaside theme, making it witty as well as pretty.

bargains below far left

Boxes of inexpensive crockery await the bargain hunter at New York store Fish's Eddy.

user friendly right

Flea-market finds are not just for show—use them for everyday meals and you'll appreciate them to the fullest.

your bathroom and bedroom. Similarly, bottles and jars that were discarded years ago when the milk, medicine, or ginger ale ran out often find their way back into the home via yard sales and estate sales. Use them to display a single flower stem or line them up en masse on a windowsill. Colored glass looks particularly good when it filters shafts of sunlight beside a window, so search for old bottles in vivid shades of cobalt blue, soft aqua, deep green, or glowing amber. Embossed lettering and original labels, plus lids, stoppers, and corks, add to their charm.

63

simple flowers **below**

The plainest glassware often makes the prettiest floral arrangements. Display single stems in some clear tumblers.

big is beautiful **below**

Oversized containers are perfect for large flowers. The narrow neck of this demi-john easily supports a huge allium.

cocktail kitsch **right**

Plastic 1950s glamour girl swizzle sticks are a perfect match for these modern classic tumblers.

rosy outlook **far right**

For impromptu displays all around the house fill cut-glass tumblers with seasonal flowers.

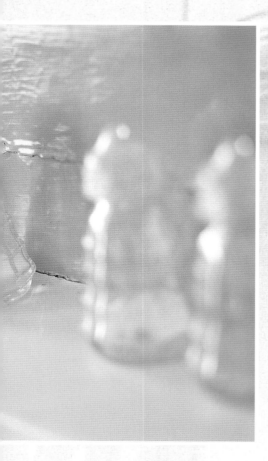

season to taste left

A row of inexpensive salt shakers makes an unpretentious and eye-catching display on a kitchen shelf in a seaside home.

high life below

Old glass bottles with their original spring-loaded stoppers take pride of place on top of a cupboard.

blue mood above left

An antique cachepot is now home to a simple display of backyard flowers.

in bloom left/far left

Antiques and flowers are combined in Potted Gardens, a New York florist's store.

lock and key right

Junk collections are about style, not cost. This array of old lock barrels has esthetic rather than monetary value.

on show left

The possessions that fill a house reflect the owner's character and interests—the contents of artist Yuri Kuper's converted barn in Normandy reveal his fondess for architectural prints and a variety of found objects ranging from a pestle and mortar to a pair of discarded boots.

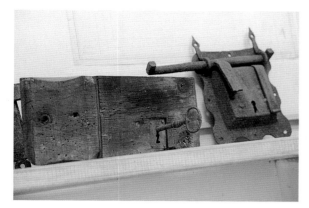

collections
and collectibles

Anything can provide the starting point for a collection of junk objects, from an array of old tobacco tins to a handful of lead fishing weights. Once you have chanced upon something you covet, every subsequent trip to a junk store thereafter will have more significance because it might reveal just the thing you have been looking for. A collection speaks volumes about the person who has amassed it, and quirky and highly idiosyncratic items often become the most obsessively sought. The hunt for picture books, pearl buttons, board games, egg whisks, hats, or birdcages can become all-consuming, and when displayed around the house, these objects add lovely witty touches.

beside the sea right

This collection of fishing weights

turned up in a local thrift store.

tinware **right**

This group of battered tins is on show in Yuri Kuper's loft apartment in New York.

garden shed **below**

The best collector's items may be lying forgotten in a shed; search out bell jars, pots, and watering-can sprinklers.

More everyday objects are also worth searching for. Kitchenware is a perennial favorite, and some covetable household utensils, such as kettles and weighing scales, can earn their keep as well as enlarge your collection if they are still in working order. Garden tools are another popular option, especially old trowels, terra-cotta pots, and baskets, which can either adorn a sunroom or be pressed back into service.

But not everyone who spends hours searching for the perfect piece to add to his or her collection ends up with a house full of clutter. Collecting can be compatible with a desire for a more minimal interior. But whatever look you want to create, be precise about what you are looking for: Discretion and theming are the keys to making discerning purchases from the myriad junk available.

handiwork **left**

Tools become decorative items in their own right when hung on the wall; the more evidence of use the better.

flat out **above**

Discerning collectors focus their attention on one item—such as antique flat irons—and look for additions wherever they go.

in stitches **right**

A still life is created from a collection of old sewing para- phernalia—much still in its original delightful packaging.

a cut above **below**

Show off your treasures behind glass—dressmaker's tools and a tape measure go on display in two handsome jars.

well spun **above**

The natural hues of these old silk threads, some still threaded on factory-size spools, form another haber-dashery-inspired collection.

hat stand

An old fruit-picking ladder is used to display a collection of straw hats in artist Charlotte Culot's Provençal home.

outside interest far left

Multicolored plaster-relief plaques decorate the walls of an outbuilding at Ruby Beet's store on Long Island.

ultra marine left

Flying birds, a wooden sailing boat, and a model fish create a distinctly nautical display in a seaside home.

still life below

Dried seed heads, ceramics, pictures, and shells are the simple ingredients that bring a shelf to life.

decoration
and display

Finding ways to arrange the items you have collected from junk stores is great fun. The more innovative and creative your displays the better, as they invite you to look at old objects in a new light as well as allow you to decorate your home with an interesting and personal touch. For small-scale arrangements, corner cabinets, narrow wooden shelves, small cubbyholes, and old wooden printer's type boxes are tailor-made. Displays of belongings make a room feel lived in, so keep them fresh by changing them whenever the mood takes you—or when a buying trip forces you to make room for another irresistible treasure.

Look out for glazed box frames and glass-fronted cabinets to show off tiny trinkets. Bigger items, especially in the kitchen and the pantry, can be hung from ceiling racks and wooden clothes dryers. Some successful displays arrange like with like so you can enjoy their similarities: Imagine the effect of seeing a row of identical clear-glass apothecary jars on a bathroom cabinet or a shelf of spongeware pitchers. Others work well because of the deliberate juxtaposition of different styles, colors, and textures. You might love the contrast between contemporary ceramics and old porcelain, or artificial flowers and brass candlesticks.

three of a kind **above**

Simple wooden shovels are propped up against the wood-panel wall of a beach house.

holy orders **left**

Religious icons fill a shrine-like wooden cupboard in a home in Amsterdam.

gallery **right/overleaf**

A rusty saw embellished with wonderful lettering has been given pride of place on a white wall, while treasures varying from a lifebuoy to a battered old shoe last are used as adornment (next page).

beach finds **above**

Use the finds from your beachcombing expeditions to cover a selection of boxes.

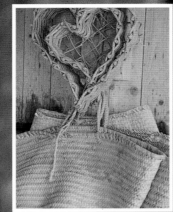

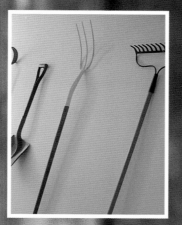

found objects

Junk addicts keep an eye out for objects of interest wherever they go. Whether you are spending a lazy day on a beach, digging in a flowerbed, or out on a woodland walk, there's a good chance that you might discover a natural wonder or some long-ago discarded man-made object that can become a treasure in its own right. It is particularly satisfying to collect these things as they are close at hand, easy to find, and—best of all—absolutely free. Beachcombing can be as much fun for children discovering the joys of the beach for the first time as it is for adults recapturing

natural selection **above**

A walk in the woods can turn up natural finds such as feathers and textural stones.

mantelpiece **right**

These skulls were found in the Camargue and in Africa, while the antlers are from Provence.

wooden wonders **above**

Interesting pieces of driftwood,
wooden bowls, and undressed
stone surfaces provide a natural
look in a bathroom.

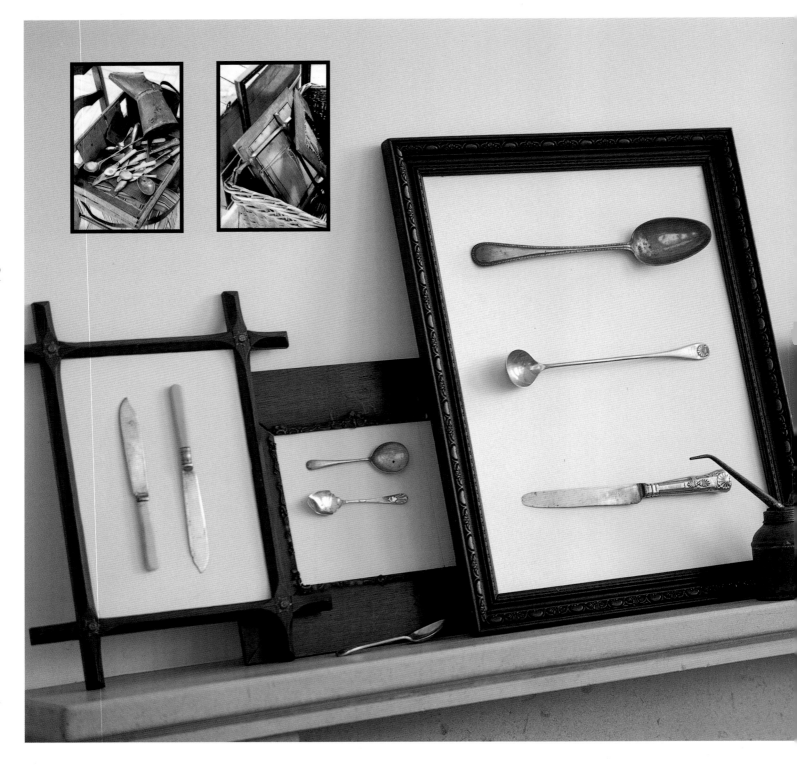

in the frame **left**

*Odd pieces of flatware find a
new home mounted on white
cardboard and displayed in
secondhand frames.*

in full bloom **right**

*An old wooden barrow,
complete with the original
wheel, has been permanantly
parked and planted to make
an unusual container garden.*

81

childhood memories. Scan the high-water mark, and you might
find jewellike pieces of sea-smoothed glass washed up alongside
delicate feathers, gnarled and twisted lengths of driftwood,
chunks of flint, and maybe a lobster pot or a float.

As they turn over the soil, gardeners—particularly owners of
old houses—are accustomed to unearthing a wealth of interesting objects. Fragments of pottery, perhaps a section of glazed
tile, a cup handle, or a section of clay pipe are all worth keeping.
In addition to being beautifully made and lovely to look at, these
objects can also be give a fascinating insight into the local history
of the area in which you live. Elsewhere in the yard, old flowerpots and wrought-iron brackets are waiting to be discovered and
appreciated. Luckier finds are discarded garden tools, such as
rusted rakes and shovels, or even an old wheelbarrow. These can
be turned into permanent decorative outdoor features or even
brought into the house to be shown off.

hidden potential **above**

*Another wheelbarrow sits
in an outbuilding awaiting a
similar transformation.*

pots of color **above**

Mottle-glazed ceramic pots are ideal for holding all sorts of floral specimens—short or tall.

indoor garden **above**

Bring terra-cotta pots in from the potting shed and enjoy the flowers while they bloom.

flowers

A vase of fresh flowers gives instant warmth to a room filled with junk furniture. Flawless and relatively short-lived, floral arrangements provide a graceful counterpoint to the imperfections and timelessness of old furniture. The vivid shades introduce a note of intense color that will lift the spirits, and such an injection of vitality can be particularly welcome in neutral room schemes.

formal or informal **left/above**

A stemmed bowl is a perfect centerpiece, while a metal jug is more casual.

growing interest above

Nature has taken over a rusty
metal garden chair.

delicate touch left

Plain shapes and clear glass
are best for simple flowers.

new life left

An old metal kettle is now home to a cluster of cheerful pansies; an enameled jug plays host to hydrangeas.

spike below

Who says plants thrive only in clay pots? They will be happy in all manner of containers, given proper drainage holes.

pitcher perfect **below**

Place sprays of the same type of flower in different vases and place them near each other for a charming group.

well contained **right**

Junk finds such as these buckets make perfect vases— the more unexpected the container the better.

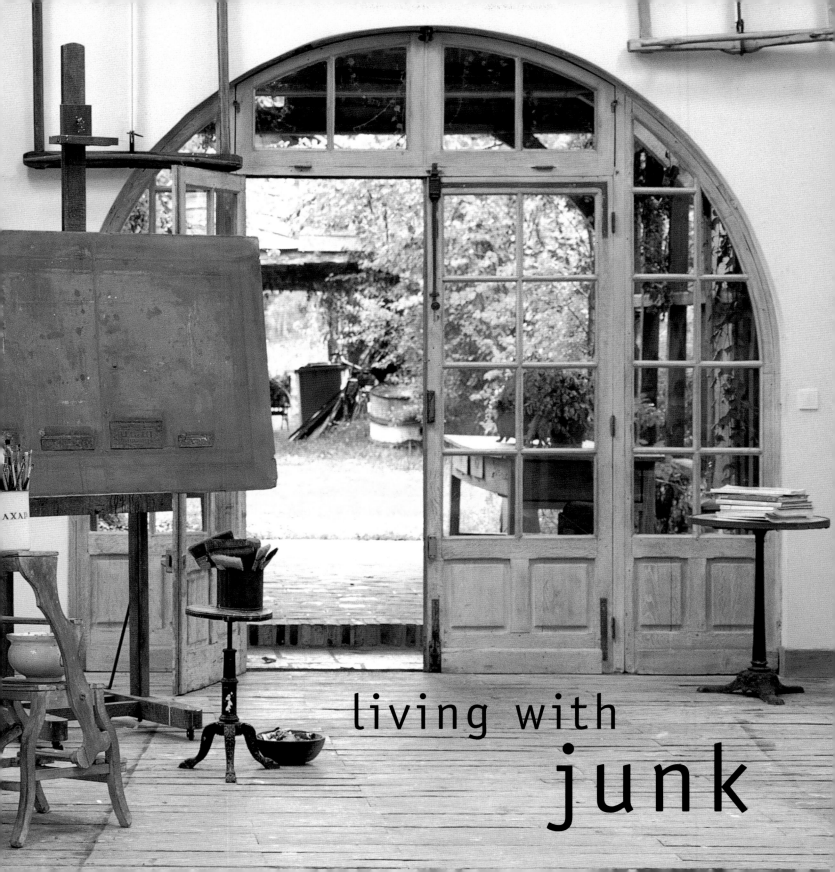

living with
junk

classics left

Twentieth-century classic Corbusier-designed chairs mingle happily with more humble flea-market furniture in a Paris apartment.

living
and dining

Once you have tracked down the best secondhand furniture, fabrics, and accessories you can find, it's time to put all the elements together to create a home that looks good and is easy to live in. There are no rules—no strictures about making exact matches or even about using items for the purpose they were originally designed. One of the pleasure of using junk is that pieces salvaged from a former life bring some of that character with them—but junk style is not a wallow in nostalgia or about faithfully recreating replicas of historical interiors. It is a look that is very much of the moment.

back to basics right

Decoration is minimal in this restored 17th-century grain store—just the Duke of Gloucester's old picnic hamper adorns the wall.

living with junk

Junk-style interiors are fresh and modern. The less clutter there is around, the better able you are to appreciate the clean lines of chairs and tables chosen for their strong shapes and design. Often it is a particular color or texture that will have attracted you to a secondhand item in the first place, whether it's the glow of wood patinated with the scars of previous use or the jewellike shine of colored glass, so you will want to show off your finds to their best advantage. Spontaneity

keeping it simple

A rough garden spade decorates the wall of Yuri Kuper's New York loft, left. Here, a large old pine table with a collection of mismatched chairs is well-placed to enjoy the canal view in Amsterdam.

92

and a lack of pretension are at the heart of junk style. Whatever pieces you find will speak for themselves, establishing their own unique style and making everyone who enters your living space feel completely and utterly at home.

For a light and spacious look with wonderfully restrained adornment, decorate your living and dining areas with plain white walls and just a few selected treasures. For a busier effect, paint it in rich shades and introduce the paintings, ornate mirrors, and quirky objects that you have picked up over the years. If there is space in your living room for two or even three sofas,

long table **left**

Charlotte Culot bought her generously proportioned dining table from a flea market in Ardeche.

rural retreat **far left**

Peter Hone's country home, a 17th-century grain store, is furnished with a charming hodgepodge of finds.

eating out **below**

Restoration was kept to a minimum when stylish restaurant Wooloomooloo in Avignon was converted from an old printing factory.

so much the better. Arrange them facing each other, perhaps alongside some slouchy armchairs, to make a sociable grouping. Despite the variety of shapes, sizes, and different colors and design of the worn upholstery fabrics, the room will feel harmonious as each of the elements in it is laid back and unaffected.

If you are lucky enough to have a fireplace, make it the room's focus by centering your sofas and chairs around it. Look for old fireirons, screens, metal fenders, and coal scuttles to set in the hearth to complete the picture. Other junk purchases, such as low footstools and occasional tables, are good for adding extra

on the bench left

Long benches, whether old garden furniture or even church pews, are wonderfully versatile in dining rooms because they can seat so many people.

wood right

The beauty of wooden furniture is that whatever type of wood it is, from pine to oak, and whatever the colour, it will always look good with other wooden furniture.

comfort and convenience, along with an assortment of feather-filled scatter cushions, colorful throws, and warm tartan blankets. Look out for rag mats and woven hearth rugs to give the room yet another layer of softness.

Whether you have a separate dining area or tend to eat in the family room or kitchen, every house should have a special place set aside for the enjoyment of food, from family lunches to dinner with friends. Junk style creates a warm and inviting look that is a far cry from the stuffiness of a formal dining room. No one has to stand on ceremony because the table is rough-and-ready pine rather than polished mahogany, the candlesticks are hand-blown glass rather than solid silver, and the tablecloth is not starched white damask but a simple length of gingham check. Table settings can be as plain or as ornate as you like—even at its most decorative, junk is never overwhelming. At one end of the spectrum, create a no-frills approach with a bare wooden tabletop set with plain white china in a mixture of weights and shapes, linen napkins, plain stainess-steel flatware, chunky glasses, and a pitcher of flowers. For more special occasions, old lace can form the backdrop for floral china, bone-handled silver flatware, cut-glass goblets, and a stemmed crystal dish piled high with fruit.

kitchens

People tend to gather in the kitchen because it is a place of warmth, a place where they can go to enjoy good company as well as nourishment, where conversations, meals, work, food preparation, and leisure activities can all happily take place alongside one another.

take a seat opposite

Sturdy church chairs, like these salvaged from a Sunday school, make excellent kitchen seating.

old kettles below

Old aluminum kettles and colanders can be found in abundance and look great.

pots and pans far left

This matching set of aluminum saucepans with white handles was found in a Paris flea market.

Kitchen junk looks at home even in a contemporary setting. It makes a lovely contrast to stainless-steel stoves and built-in cabinets, and gives authenticity to retro kitchens inspired by, for example, '40s or '50s style. You might find yourself being more selective and choosing fewer pieces than you would for a country-style kitchen, but the junk elements you do include will really stand out against the room's cool, clean lines.

Though kitchen gadgets are now incredibly sophisticated, it can be great fun to scour markets and auction rooms in search of early examples of this technology. Pieces from decades ago, such as meat mincers, coffee grinders, juicers, nutcrackers, ice cream makers, and weighing scales with their sets of brass or iron weights, were often so well designed and sturdily built that they are still going strong today. Not only are they better looking than many of today's plastic or electronic gadgets, yesterday's household goods are also far more satisfying to use. Old utensils have similar esthetic advantages. Sets of saucepans, tiny metal tea

retro chic left

Designer Roxanne Beis loved the 1940s cupboards she inherited with her Paris apartment so much she designed her kitchen around them.

strainers, enameled colanders, ladles, spatulas, rolling pins, and strainers can be suspended from a kitchen shelf to keep them always at hand. Keep an eye out for any other hardware that would add character to your kitchen, from thermometers, trays, and canisters to mops, buckets, and brooms.

heart of the home above

Painter Charlotte Culot bought her old range from a local village in Provence. The charcoal-burning stove with its long ventilator pipe keeps out winter chill.

If you want a traditional country kitchen, enhance the reassuringly familiar look by adding an old refectory table, some unpainted wooden cupboards, a few plain rush-seated chairs or long benches, and the most basic floor covering you can find: bare boards, terra-cotta tiles, or rush matting are perfect. Keep the look as uncomplicated and utilitarian as possible. Wooden utensils and copper pans can be hung up for decoration (though any sign of damage means they are not safe to actually cook with), and old stove-top kettles, salt-glazed storage jars, and chunky earthenware pottery can be stowed on open shelves until needed. Secondhand ranges are prized for their warmth, good looks, and efficiency, but prices tend to reflect the keen

whistling kettle right

A portable single gas burner is just the right size to boil up a tuneful cup of tea.

back to basics left

This simply furnished barn deep in the Dutch countryside takes guests back to simpler times.

101

demand for machines in sound working condition, so always seek the advice of a qualified professional before having one installed to make sure your money is being well spent.

For a slightly more sophisticated kitchen, a different sort of junk sets the tone. Choose an old ceramic sink and simple pieces of furniture painted in shades of warm cream, pale blue, and soft green. Tongue-and-groove wall paneling looks lovely when given the same paint treatment. Line shelves with tins and enamelware, and display an assortment of delicately patterned dishes on wall-mounted plate racks and simple cup hooks—all will contribute more to the room's overall style and mood than their modest price tag might suggest.

In addition to being decorative, old tins and cans can be restored to their original purpose and be used to store anything from dried fruit to flour. Other groceries can be stored in old meat lockers, wooden crates, baskets, galvanized buckets, and even large preserving pans. Keep cleaning materials out of sight under the sink, concealed by a curtain made by gathering some old fabric on a length of wire.

in the balance **above**

Traditional commercial scales have

a reassuringly reliable quality.

little pitchers far left

Pitchers are indispensable
around the kitchen—use them
to serve water or hold flowers.

pickled wood left

All the woodwork in this
kitchen has been "aged" with
white paint sanded smooth.

labeled up above

Any lettering on an object,
especially foreign, can add
considerably to its charm.

old and new left

A quirky collection of old baskets and containers adds character to modern kitchen equipment and cabinets.

a unified whole right

An accumulation of interesting finds has been put together in this kitchen to create a room full of character.

good service below

The best junk finds earn their keep by being functional as well as looking good.

display

*This beautifully battered linen
closet was painted to match the
monochrome bedroom.*

bedrooms

Your bedroom should be more relaxed and comfortable than any other room of the house. Filling it with junk-store discoveries will strike just the right balance between indulgence and simplicity. Imagine a plain wrought-iron bed made up with white cotton sheets and covered with a downy quilt, and you'll appreciate the essence of this style.

overwrought **above**

This ornate iron bed came from a Belgian flea market. The white linen was found closer to its Provence home in the famous Isle sur la Sorgue market.

old linen **above**

Simple bed linen with just a hint of decoration is the best dressing for an ornate bed.

brassed off **above/right**

Check out painted metal bedsteads carefully—you might find brass hidden beneath.

field of dreams left

Large furniture sales are the best places to go if you want to choose from a range of antique beds in one place. But be prepared to transport your bulky purchase home if you do succumb to temptation.

Battered antique bedsteads appear in all the usual junk-lovers' haunts, and each will set a slightly different mood and style for your bedroom. Sometimes headboards are available together with their bases, mattresses, or footboards, sometimes without. However, don't pass over a beautiful find just because it's incomplete, as separate bases and mattresses can easily be bought or made to fit. Falling in love with the headboard itself is the most important thing. Remember, too, that the most unusual junk-store finds can be adapted to make headboards—gates, plank doors, and carved panels can all be cut to size and attached to a base, so keep your mind open to such possibilities while you are on your search.

dormitory right

When the owner of this home—a former boarding school—moved in, she found these old iron school beds left behind. You should find similar ones in salvage yards, or look for announcements in local papers that a local school or nursing home is closing down.

gateway **opposite**

Think beyond the obvious for bedroom furniture. Weathered wooden gates can make quirky head- and footboards.

well handled **below**

Don't be too finicky about cleaning up your find. Fittings, such as handles, and flaking paint add to the charm.

Simple metal-framed hospital and dormitory beds are good for children because they are so sturdy, while more decorative wrought-iron versions—twins or doubles—are ideal for guest rooms. Showier and more intricate designs—perhaps a *lit bateau* or a bed with brass knobs—might be worth reserving for the master bedroom, where a hint of grandeur will be beautifully offset by the room's more humble elements. A romantic four-poster is a rare junk find, but you could make your own version using reclaimed or recycled wooden supports and draping them with plain white voile.

The bedroom is a good place to mix old with new: the charm of an old frame with the comfort of a modern mattress, or a vintage cotton cover on a new comforter. When you are buying new pillows, bolsters, and quilts, opt for ones that are filled in the traditional manner with duck feathers or, better still, goose down.

Bedroom furniture can be as minimal or as decorative as you like. Near-empty rooms that contain just a bed make a dramatic statement and are somehow deeply appealing. But bear in mind that the peace and tranquility of this sort of space will quickly be shattered by too much clutter, so avoid this look unless you are impeccably neat, own very few possessions, or have space for a separate dressing room. A less austere solution is to add a few pieces of junk furniture. Store clothes in a wooden armoire, as large as you have space for, a chest of drawers or a linen chest, or alternatively on a commercial metal clothes rack bought from a wholesale supplier or picked up in a junk sale. When looking for bedside tables, think beyond conventional cabinets and use small round metal café tables, wooden stools, or metal seats to keep your water glass and nighttime reading close at hand.

original features left

This bedroom is in a house that dates from 1520. The walls have been left virtually as they were found after 30 years of neglect, when the present owners moved in.

traveling bed right

Peter Hone found this 1860s traveling bed in an antiques shop in Devon, England. It came with an array of baggage labels collected during its days of being shunted around on trains with an earlier owner.

bathrooms

Reclaimed antique bathroom fixtures have serious appeal to junk shoppers. In comparison to flimsy modern acrylic versions, cast-iron rolltop claw-foot baths are far superior. The same goes for old porcelain sinks set in metal stands, huge chrome daisy-head shower attachments, and Victorian toilets with their original high-mounted cisterns. And a few small touches can make all the difference to existing plain white fixtures: Swap the faucets for reconditioned originals, add some down-to-earth junk-style accessories, whitewash the walls, and all that remains for you to do is turn on the water, lie back, and relax.

bathing in style right

This bath traveled on the top of a car from a Brussels flea market to its home in Provence. It now takes pride of place in this spectacular bathroom. An old wooden frame found on a farm has become a quirky towel rack.

shattered glass left

A fragment of mirror perched on the faucets is all that's needed.

safely stored

Bathrooms are ideal places for showing
all those wonderful pieces of china
you've collected. A classic white jug will
find a home anywhere, while pretty
plates are useful for holding small
items of bathroom paraphernalia.

Infinite variety is available to those who search architectural salvage yards and specialized outlets at home and abroad in pursuit of something unique. Stumbling on an old bathtub used as a cattle trough in the middle of a field is less likely to happen these days, but you might get lucky. Re-enameling is always possible if it is otherwise in good shape.

Devotees of junk style don't mind having a sink, bathtub, and toilet that don't match, and won't object to using a garden table as a washstand, so long as the spirit of casual simplicity reigns. Mix styles, designs, and functions according to what's available and what looks best.

Once you have established the look of the room with its main fixtures, try to keep everything else as uncluttered and as simple as possible. Bathrooms need a surprising amount of storage space in order to maintain their clean lines. Pieces of furniture imported from elsewhere in the house can all find a home here: Store toiletries in a spare kitchen cabinet, hang bathrobes on a peg rack brought up from the pantry, or pile towels into an empty blanket chest from the bedroom.

Traditional-style items of bathroom furniture are as useful as ever, so when you go shopping, keep an eye out for old lockable medicine chests, small mirrored cabinets, and tile-backed washstands. For authenticity's sake, combine them with a porcelain or enameled pitcher and bowl set and piles of embroidered cotton handtowels. Classic bathroom accessories, such as glass shelves, mirrors, shaving mugs, toothbrush holders, soap dishes, and chunky chrome towel racks, also appear from time to time in flea markets. Otherwise, improvise with a piece of

---

light and airy **above**

A charming basin has been tucked into the eaves of this Normandy barn. The mirror has been unceremoniously sliced to neatly fit the space.

driftwood as a bathroom shelf, a gold-framed hall mirror above the sink, an old glass tumbler to hold the toothbrushes, a floral-patterned china saucer as a soap dish, or a basic wooden trestle as a towel rack. Similarly, if you can't find a bath mat made the old-fashioned way from cork or wooden duckboard slats , use a small hearth rug instead.

Flowers will give as much pleasure in the bathroom as they do in any other room in the house, so remember to place a small vase on the washstand or on the bathroom shelf, and hang up a bunch of lavender to keep the air fresh and sweet-smelling. Together, such small details will enhance the sensual pleasure of your bathroom for you and your guests.

118

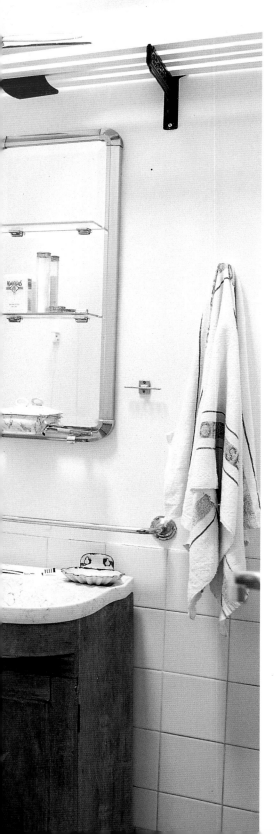

119

nautical sink far left

*This seaside junk-store buy was
once owned by a sea captain.*

all at sea left

*Toy ships from a warehouse
give a seagoing theme.*

salvaged above

*With a little work, enameled
sinks can be restored to life.*

soap stars far left

Enamelware dishes come in all
shapes, even shells. Lettering
makes them more collectible.

crossed wires above left

Twisted metalwork containers are
ideal for bathroom storage—
excess water will drain away.

sinking feeling left

Look for unusually shaped basins
—industrial designs are more
interesting than domestic.

reinvention above

This lovely enameled ashtray
is far more suitably employed
holding blocks of soap.

trough **above/right**

The unusually deep bath in this elegant paneled bathroom is actually a cattle trough that was found abandoned in a Lincolnshire field. The wooden feet were made especially to support it, and the faucets have been fixed to the wall to avoid damaging the trough.

ship ahoy **far right**

White painted walls and tiles maximize the light from an old ship's lamp—a characterful accent in a bathroom.

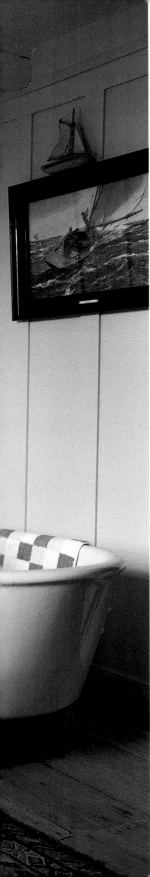

workrooms,
studies, and studios

workstation

Surround yourself with stylish accessories while you work to create an atmosphere conducive to concentration.

Whether you run a business from home or just need somewhere peaceful to write letters, pay bills, pursue hobbies, or store papers, a workspace is essential. Filling your study with modern office furniture would make it efficient, neat, and well organized, but its dull uniformity and lack of character would leave much to be desired. Turn instead to junk and you will be able to create a workspace with style, flair, and a distinctly human touch. Even in the most minimal environment, a few quirky and characterful pieces of furniture will be inspirational. First, choose a location. If you are lucky enough to have a whole room at your disposal, it's relatively easy to create a businesslike workspace—there's also the advantage of being able to shut the door on everything at the end of the day. For a rather less spacious office, but one that can still accommodate a small writing table, use part of a wide landing or the corner of a bedroom or dining room. If you select your furniture and accessories with as much care as you would take in choosing items for the rest of your home, a workspace will not jar in the context of your other furnishings but blend in seamlessly with the area in which you live and relax.

First on your shopping list will be a worktable. An old rolltop desk is ideal, especially one with lots of built-in drawers, letter racks, and penholders. But this sort of piece can be expensive, and often a simple kitchen table or console will do just as well. If your studio is used for crafts or practical work, like painting or sewing, a large wooden trestle—or even an old door resting on two low cupboards—will more than suffice.

A comfortable seat, ideally one that is adjustable and offers good back support, is your next priority. Why not look out for chairs that were originally intended for office use? It seems an appropriate form of recycling to return furniture like this to its original function. And by its very nature, good office furniure will

126

window seat left

A small folding table makes the most of the natural light that streams in through a dormer window.

space to spare above

This journalist's office is kept as deliberately spare as possible, with an old typewriter in place of a computer.

have been designed for comfort in use. Find out when office-furniture clearance sales are taking place in your area, but also scout sales and auctions for older styles, such as tall adjustable architect's chairs with low back supports and wooden swivel chairs on castors—they still look great, and their classic clean lines work perfectly in a contemporary junk-style environment.

You'll need to adopt some ingenious storage solutions to keep documents, books, stationery, materials, and equipment in good order—especially if space is a premium. Many people also find that they work best in uncluttered surroundings. Shelving is essential—whether you use lengths of bare plank supported by some old bricks, or find a cheap bookcase in a junk store, but office-furniture clearance sales are also excellent sources for pieces such as solid wood filing cabinets, plain metal drawer units, large map chests, and old metal lockers. For smaller scale organization, use an old vase for a pen holder, baskets as in-trays, leather trunks for filing paperwork, and hatboxes for stowing any other odds and ends.

There's not much you can do to disguise the unattractive look of equipment such as faxes and computers, but a reconditioned Bakelite telephone or an

old typewriter will help redress the balance and prevent high-tech styling taking over completely. Adjustable gooseneck desk lamps, also reminiscent of another era, are still an extremely practical and stylish option for all kinds of close work.

work with a view above

The most ordinary wooden table can become an inviting desk. Drawers are a useful feature for storing small stationery.

sunrooms
and greenhouses

128

potted history **below left**

*Timeworn wood, terra-cotta, clay,
and painted brick give a potting
shed traditional appeal.*

A sense of the natural world, with its wonderful colors and scents and its graceful dust and decay, is the overwhelming atmosphere in a greenhouse. Carry an old wooden bench out here to work on—it can double as a makeshift dining table in the cooler months when the yard is out of bounds. Gather old gardening tools and either hang them from hooks and nails or lean them in a corner ready for use. Along with the plants, work-smoothed baskets, gardening gloves, shears, shovels, spades, and forks are the only decorations your sunroom needs.

inside out **below**

This outbuilding-turned-garden room is filled with plants, ladders, pots, and straw hats in wonderfully organized chaos.

under glass **above**

A flourishing potting shed can be a place for activity as well as for relaxation.

terra-cotta **left**

Nicer than any modern counterpart, old flowerpots proliferate at tailgate and yard sales.

old world **above/below**

A covered studio adjacent to a converted barn is filled with weathered furniture and the artist-owner's own canvasses.

benchmark **right**

Redolent of traditional skills, even the most ordinary work-bench can become an understated decorative feature.

looking in **far right**

The barn is set in an orchard; plenty of greenery, both inside and out, gives it a subdued and romantic atmosphere.

living
outdoors

Any patch of yard, however small, can become an outdoor haven in good weather. Even a narrow balcony or the smallest paved area beside the back door is room enough for a small marble-topped table and white-painted metal chairs where you can eat breakfast or lunch on a summer's day. Furnish it accordingly, treating it to the same care and making use of junk style just as you do inside the house. And just as you can happily use garden furniture indoors, by the same

summer life right

A semicovered area sheltered from the elements is used as a seasonal dining room.

al fresco left/far right

Take lunch in the shade of a leafy tree or set the table for dinner. Hurricane lamps can provide light as dusk falls.

token you can transfer furniture originally designed for the home

to an outdoor setting. The effects of aging, such a key part of the

appeal of junk style, are accelerated when furniture is directly

exposed to the harsh rigors of the elements. And if you've picked

up an old table and some chairs at relatively little cost, you are

not going to be too upset when the paint blisters or lichen make

their home in the cracks of bare wood. Even fabrics can be left to

take their chances, like deck-chair canvas allowed to bleach in

the sun until its gaudy stripes have faded to shadows.

outdoor display above

Outdoor ornamentation takes many forms, from the pleasingly practical to the purely decorative. Visible signs of decay are an optional extra,

a dog's life below left

Even your animals can enjoy the benefits of junk style. This contented canine surveys outdoor activities from the comfort of a blanket-lined basket.

time for tea below left

Outdoor furniture should not be too delicate—choose
pieces that will withstand the odd shower and their
weathered look will add to the sense of informality.

daybed below

Piled with pillows and blankets to soften the hard metal,
an ironwork lounger makes a quiet place to relax and
enjoy the scenery.

back to nature below/opposite

Lunch is served outside in a specially chosen part of the orchard surrounding Yuri Kuper's house. The tables and chairs are his own designs, their wooden surfaces allowed to mellow with age and a covering of lichen.

abandoned in situ right

A forgotten plow lies rusting in a field, a reminder of a bygone age.

One of greatest pleasures of outdoor living is dining outside, and it can also be one of the most enjoyable ways of relaxing with friends. Choose a sheltered position for your garden table and chairs—this could be on the lawn, in a clearing in a corner of the yard, or closer to the house on a terrace or veranda. To really enjoy al fresco meals even in the heat of the midday sun make sure there is some shade available—an old parasol, a canopy of vines, or a shady tree will all do the job.

Junk dining furniture made from metal, rattan, wicker, or wood is ideal. If it is slightly faded, rusted, or weather-worn to start with, so much the better. Either leave a wooden tabletop on show or throw a simple checked cloth or an old white sheet over it, adding generously filled pitchers of

137

138

garden flowers to capture the lazy mood of high summer. Add plenty of soft pillows covered in easygoing cotton if chairs aren't as comfortable as they might be—you could make oversized covers from an assortment of remnants and keep a spare set to wrap around your living-room pillows. Set the table with the same pieces you would use for indoor dining. None of your robust glass tumblers, flea-market china plates, worn linen napkins, or odd pieces of flatware is too precious for a trip outdoors, and all are far nicer than plastic knives and forks or paper plates and cups. To allow your guests to enjoy the occasion far into the evening, hang hurricane lamps and storm lanterns in the trees and light them as dusk falls. Cheaper and easier still are old jars with a plain white candle inside, protected from any stray breezes.

Life outdoors proves how versatile and easygoing junk style can be. Who would swap the ease with which possessions can be transferred from house to garden and back again for the restrictions and tensions of conventional living?

sea view **above**

When you live this close to the sea the beach becomes your yard, so try to use sympathetic materials such as reclaimed wood.

a breath of fresh air

left/below

Traditional wooden deck chairs
covered in unbleached canvas
allow visitors to enjoy the sea
breeze in comfort and style.

sources

MARKETS AND FAIRS

When traveling, call the area Chamber of Commerce for information about local flea markets.

Aloha Flea Market
9500 Salt Lake Boulevard (in the parking lot of Aloha Stadium)
Honolulu, HA
tel: 808-730-9611
Held every Wednesday, Saturday, and Sunday, rain or shine. For more than 20 years, this outdoor market has catered to the eclectic tastes of America's westernmost residents and their visitors.

All-American Trade Day
11190 U.S. Highway 413 (between Albertville and Gunterville)
Gunterville, AL
tel: 205-891-2790
Held weekends all year. In addition to collectibles, this indoor and outdoor market sells livestock, poultry, and fresh produce.

American Park'n'Swap
40th Street and Washington Street
Phoenix, AZ
tel: 602-273-1258
Held every Wednesday evening, Friday, Saturday, and Sunday. The slogan at this large market is "everything you can think of from A to Z" and it is true!

Anderson Jockey Lot and Farmer's Market
Highway 29 between Greenville and Anderson
Anderson, SC
tel: 864-224-2027
Every weekend, rain or shine, 1500 to 2000 vendors spread their wares over 65 acres. As the name suggests you'll find produce and livestock as well as all sorts of vintage items.

The Annex Antiques Fair and Flea Market
Sixth Avenue between 24th and 26th Streets
New York, NY
tel: 212-243-5343
Two work-a-day parking lots turn into flea markets every Saturday and Sunday all year long. Other lots, indoors and out, have joined the bandwagon and the whole area blossoms with vintage and antique stuff on weekends.

Brimfield Antiques and Collectibles
Route 20
Brimfield, MA
tel: 413-245-3436
Held first week of May, July, and September. Dealers come from all over—including Europe—bringing everything from large pieces of furniture to silver to vintage linens.

Broad Acres Swap Meet
2960 Las Vegas Boulevard North (at Pecos Street)
North Las Vegas, NV
tel: 702-642-3777
Held every Friday, Saturday, and Sunday all year long, this outdoor flea market is the oldest and largest in Nevada. Look for "treasures" that have relocated to the Southwest with their owners as well as local items.

Englishtown Auction Sales
90 Wilson Avenue
Englishtown, NJ
tel: 732-446-9644
Held every Saturday and Sunday all year, rain or shine. Also open on special holidays and the five days before Christmas. In operation since the 1920s and covering over 100 acres, indoors and out, you'll find items from professional dealers as well as one-time attic clearers.

The Flea Market
5225 East Platte Avenue (Highway 24)
Colorado Springs, CO
tel: 719-380-8599
Held every Saturday and Sunday year-round as well as Fridays from June through September. This outdoor market has the tang of the Old West and enough merchandise to please everyone.

Flea Market at Eastern Market
Seventh Street, SE at Eastern Market (half block from Pennsylvania Avenue on Capitol Hill)
Washinton, DC
tel: 703-534-7612
Held Sundays from March through Christmas. This 15-year-old flea market has a real old-fashioned neighborhood charm along with the international atmosphere the area provides.

Fort Lauderdale Swap Shop
Sunrise Boulevard one mile west of I-95
Fort Lauderdale, FL
tel: 954-791-7927
Held every day of the year from 6 a.m. to 6 p.m. Professional dealers and locals exhibit a wide variety of "stuff."

French Market Community Flea Market
1235 North Peters Street (Elysian Fields at the Mississippi River)

New Orleans, LA
tel: 504-596-3420
Held daily out-of-doors, weather permitting. In place since the 18th century, this market represents New Orlean's fancy but faded decorating style. It's near many of the attractions of this cosmopolitan city.

Hartville Flea Market
788 Edison (at Market)
Hartville, OH
tel: 330-277-9860
Held Mondays, Thursdays, and holiday Saturdays, April through Christmas. Look for the Amish and Mennonite food purveyors as well as dealers in all sorts of merchandise. This flea market has a real country flavor.

Hinckley Flea Market
803 Highway 48 at I-35 (look for five large red-and-white buildings)
Hinckley, MN
tel: 320-384-9911
Held the first weekend in May through the last weekend in September, this is Minnesota's most modern market. You'll find campgrounds as well as collectibles, and there's a casino nearby.

Jack Loeks' Flea Market
1400 28th Street Southwest (three miles west of Route 131, in the Studio 28 parking lot)
Grand Rapids, MI
tel: 616-532-8218
Held weekends April through October, rain or shine. For 30 years this outdoor antiques and collectibles flea market has been selling all sorts of attic treasures and soon-to-be collectibles.

Kane County Flea Market
Randall Road (between Routes 38 and 64, about 40 miles west of Chicago)
St. Charles, IL
tel: 630-377-2252
Held the first Saturday and Sunday of every month. Indoor and outdoor booths specializing in heartland antiques and collectibles.

Lakewood Antiques Market
2000 Lakewood Way
Atlanta, GA
tel: 404-622-4488
Held every Friday, Saturday, and Sunday on the second full weekend of each month. Antiques, collectibles, and rediscovered treasures are the only things featured here.

Long Beach Outdoor Antiques and Collectibles Market
Veteran Boulevard at Lakewood Boulevard
Long Beach, CA
tel: 213-655-5703
Held the third Sunday of every month. A wide variety of merchandise from regular dealers as well as private individuals.

Mary's Ole Time Swap Meet
7905 Northeast 23rd Street
Oklahoma City, OK
tel: 405-427-0051
Held every weekend year-round. For over 30 years people have been shopping at Mary's, indoors and out, rain or shine.

Metrolina Expo
7100 North Statesville Road (off I-77)
Charlotte, NC
tel: 800-824-3770
Held every Friday through Sunday year-round. For nearly three decades, this has been the area's place to search for collectibles and vintage items. Special emphasis on antiques the first weekend of each month.

Picc-a-dilly Flea Market
796 West 13th Street (Lane County Fairgrounds)
Eugene, OR
tel: 541-683-5589
Held every Sunday year-round except July and August. Call to verify specific dates. Since 1970 this flea market has attracted dealers from all over selling a wide variety of antiques and collectibles.

Redwood Swap Meet
3600 Redwood Road
Salt Lake City, UT
tel: 801-973-6060
Held every Saturday and Sunday, weather permitting. This market offers a wide variety of collectibles and vintage items.

Reningers #2 Antiques Market
740 Noble Street
Kutztown, PA
tel: 717-385-0104
Held every Saturday year-round. "Extravaganzas" are held on Saturday and Sunday in late April, late June, and late September. Call for dates. Amish, Pennsylvania Dutch, primitive, and folk art are the specialties at this long-standing and well-known flea market, but you'll find lots of everything.

The Rose Bowl Flea Market
Pasadena, CA
tel: 626-588-4411
Held the second Sunday of every month. Vintage goods from high kitsch to fine furnishings.

Saturday Market
Third and E Streets (across from the Hilton Hotel)
Anchorage, Alaska
tel: 907-276-7207
Held every Sunday from mid-May through mid-September. In addition to antiques and collectibles, new merchandise and crafts are featured as well as fresh produce in season.

Sparks Flea Market
At the junction of old U.S. Highway 36 (Mission Road) and Route 7 (about halfway between St. Joseph, MO, and Atchison, KS)
Sparks, KS
tel: 913-985-2411
Held three weekends a year: in early May, early July, and over Labor Day. Call for specific dates. This wonderful market is not only known for its antiques and collectibles but also for its superior regional food.

141

Tennessee State Fairgrounds Flea Market
Wedgewood Avenue and Nolensville Road (State Fairgrounds)
Nashville, TN
tel: 615-262-5016
Held the fourth weekend of every month, this long standing flea market is a Nashville tradition, playing host to almost 1200 vendors. Expect to find most anything.

Trader Jack's Flea Market
North of Highway 85, on the Santa Fe Opera Grounds
Santa Fe, NM
No telephone.
Held Fridays, Saturdays, and Sundays in spring, summer, and fall. Specializing in Southwestern antiques and collectibles.

Traders Village
7979 North Eldridge Parkway (3/10 mile south of I-290)
Houston, TX
tel: 281-890-5500
Held every weekend year-round. With a keen understanding of the needs of collectors, this market has, in addition to acres of "stuff," rides for the kids, cash machines, and a park for recreational vehicles.

acknowledgments

Firstly thanks to Tom Leighton for his kindness, good humor, and for always taking beautiful pictures whatever the weather, and to Simon Whitmore, his assistant, for keeping us on the right road. Also to Larraine Shamwana for her consistent encouragement and great art direction—her huge contribution to pulling this project together creatively will not be forgotten. I couldn't have asked for a better team to travel and work with.

This book would not have come together at all without the wonderful houses I've been allowed to photograph, so I'm indebted to their owners, all of whom seemed to share the same spirit and made the photography for this book so memorable: garden antiques expert Peter Hone, garden designer Arne Maynard, interior designer Philip Hooper, artist Yuri Kuper, painter Charlotte Culot, lighting designer Alexis Aufray, designers Roxanne Beis and Jean-Bernard Navier; and also Marilyn Phipps, Netty Nauta, Caroline and Michael Breet, Aleid Rontgen and Annette Brederode; Glen Senk and Keith Johnson of Anthropologie, Jim and Pat Cole of Coming to America, and George Laaland at Woolloomooloo Restaurant. I'm also grateful to the following shops for kindly allowing us to photograph their wonderful collections of secondhand furniture and accessories: **Xavier Nicod Antiquites**, 9 Avenue des Quatre, Otages, 84800 Isle sur la Sorgue, France; **Anthropologie**, 375 West Broadway, New York, NY 10012; 201 West Lancaster Avenue, Wayne, PA 19087; 11500 Rockville Pike, Rockville, MD 20852; 1365 Post Road East, Westport, CT 06880; 9 Northern Boulevard, Greenvale, NY 11548; 823 Newport Center Drive, Newport Beach, CA 92660, 1402 Third Street Promenade, Santa Monica, CA 90401; 1120 North State Street, Chicago, IL 60610; 1780 Green Bay Road, Highland Park, IL 60035; **Coming to America**, 276 Lafayette Street, New York, NY 10012; **Fishs Eddy**, 889 Broadway, New York , NY 10003 and 2176 Broadway, New York, NY 10024; **Potted Gardens**, 27 Bedford Street, New York, NY 10014 and Bridgehampton, NY 11932; **Ruby Beets Antiques**, 1703 Montauk Highway, Bridgehampton, NY 11932.

I would also like to thank all my friends and colleagues who helped me to track them down, especially Polly and Mark Gilbey in London, Roxanne Beis, and Amelie Thiodet in France, Nina Monfils in Holland and Andrea Raisfeld in New York.

Thanks to all at Ryland, Peters & Small, especially Jacqui Small for giving me this great opportunity as well as my patient and long-suffering editor Sian Parkhouse. Alice Westgate should also not go unmentioned for all her hard work. Thanks also to my sister Caroline for her translations, to Fiona Craig McFeely and Jo Tyler for their help, and to my agent Fiona Lindsay.

On a personal front, thanks to my brilliant sons, George and Ralph, for taking my too frequent absences over the summer in such good humor and, of course, Belinda for keeping things together at home. Above all, thanks to my wonderful husband, Martin, for everything.